Adrift

Andrea Phillips

Adrift © 2022 Andrea Phillips

All rights reserved.

No part of this publication may be reproduced, stored in a retrieval system, or transmitted, in any form or by any means, electronic, mechanical, photocopying, recording or otherwise, without the prior written permission of the presenters.

Andrea Phillips asserts the moral right to be identified as author of this work.

Presentation by *BookLeaf Publishing*

Web: www.bookleafpub.com

E-mail: info@bookleafpub.com

ISBN: 9789357695237

First edition 2022

*I dedicate this work to Tina and Eduardo,
Kevin and Sofia for their support and love.*

ACKNOWLEDGEMENT

I would like to thank my husband, Kevin Phillips for the love, the patience, for walking side by side and encouraging me to grow, to Ana Sofia Phillips, our beautiful, brave and curious daughter that inspires me to be a better version of myself; my friend Genivaldo Cavalcanti, for all the compassion, friendship, and encouragement with who I can share my passion for literature and music; Marcus Lucon for the provocative ideas, for the friendship and the love you always send to my way, Gabriela Klein for all the long conversations about absolutely everything, always giving me so much food for thought; for Greg Moser for offering help and for our friendship and support, for Iara Anschutz for reminding me of sunnier and brighter days. For my brother Marcos and his wife Giovana for all support and their presence in my life; for Liz Braun, Migdalia Braun and Anarosa Braun for always pouring so much unconditional love through all these years, for my friend Regina Lewis for keep remind me of my light and purpose and for my parents for making everything possible, for caring, for raising me, and for rescuing me some many times without

any judgement. Thank you Thank you Thank
you Thank you.

PREFACE

Adrift are poems about survival and perseverance.

The Game

You need to be assertive, loud and sucessful
and to be loved and envied by a number of
people.
You need to be tall and skinny
You need to be white and witty
You need to be able to bounce back
every time, all the time everywhere
You need to learn from your mistakes, and
never repeat them
You need to smile and have strong handshakes.
You need to be reliable, independent
You need to drink the Kool Aid
You need to be driven, ambitious, competitive,
A go getter, unbreakable, desirable.
You need to bury all the feelings somewhere
inside
Move to the suburbs and buy
a house with five bedrooms
finished basement and an attic
so all your demons can finally run free
somewhere
letting out a glimpse of your humanity.

P.S.: and if none of this works for you, I am sad
to say that you are a dreamer

in this case you shoud try write a novel, recite poetry, visit the art museum, listen to jazz and radiohead, read your heart out because your life depend on it. Learn how to cultivate orchids, dance whenever you feel like you should, show that you love, cry listening to George Gershwin and the Wizard of Oz, help the ones who need you, thinking that if you don't help them no one will; turn the other cheek and be ready for the pain, plant flowers, spend time with nature, be humble, spend time with Van Gogh arts, (he gets you)

P.S.S: if that does not work, I am afraid to say that nothing will.

Not going back

Trying to hold on to a piece of hope floating
at sea
and to be saved by a hair of your sympathy
On sight
Lost in my own world
Muted by my own words
Hurt by my self inflicted wounds
Defeated with my own sword
I skinned off my face with my own hands
I wanted you to see the level of my pain
I wanted you to understand when I was not able
to go on.
If you give yourself too much there is nothing
left.
Not a hair
Nor safe shores
Not going back
Not a piece of hope floating
Not a hand to pull me out of my day terrors
Not a detour to the route taking me to
where I was a dreamer
If you give yourself too much, there is nothing
left.

Madness

Madness is a castle at 10 inches off the ground
If You lost touch with the forces that hold you
grounded you are there,
That is all it takes.
Madness is warm at times
It has inviting open doors to all of us
that closes like fists once you are in
Open windows that attract all kinds of flying
creatures
Birds and dragonflies
you can dance on its empty rooms with your
imaginary partners
you can finger drawing in the air and erase it
with the palm of your hands
10 inches off the ground
It is all it takes and once you are there, there you
are.
And no going back.

Left and right

5

You wanted me to change and I stood in silence
wanting to see change on you.
We are both right in our own ways, we both
wrong in our own ways
It turns out we are fighting the same monster, on
the opposite side of its stomach,
We're both been swallowed, both of us, it
gobbled us up, it stepped on us,
To be vomited eventually
Eight to five, twenty five to life.
No parole for no one.

Time is an entity

One second after the disaster, encompasses all
the disaster
one second after death is eternal death
I don't know when the end started
I know enough to wish I could stop one minute
before the explosion.
one second after the shock
one minute after the shame
the shot of adrenaline
the realisation that nothing will return to its
what was known
the emptiness after pondering that the old house
is no longer yours
you shall not go back to the backyard of the
early years
and you should not go back to those friends
the sunday afternoons are over and the sun
cast a shadows over different buildings now
somedays I sit and breath on the very second
before the disaster
holding my hands against my ears
waiting for you to say those words
that burnt the mask that covered your face.
I have lived this scene so many times in my head

time that insists on throw me to the future or the
void that came after the turning point
Time is an entity.

Disease

At the end of every road there is an abyss
as if I was born to fall
yet I try to hold on to something,
and to create a new story prior to the end
my best and my worst are the same now
or maybe I am not able to discern
I come back to the same ruins in circles
ad infinitum
I leave
to return all over again.

The boat

9

I am a boat in the middle of the ocean
adrift
just hoping that the water is the hand of God
that will save me from myself.

The Noun

I write mostly to suppress my loneliness
to feel a little more connected...
I understand that everything I feel has got to
have a name
but they don't have a name yet for it.
I need to bring them to light
casting them out of my shadows,
maybe someone out there can name it,
even if it is my own name.

Grinding

He broke one rule that could have cost his job
and losing a paycheck would result losing the
roof,
losing the hope, breaking the rule could have
cost him an arm.
and he was willing to pay the price.
A full grown man sitting on a chair almost
crying
almost begin "am I going to lose my job" ?
when he could have lost his arm,
Those machines are heavy, they can harm.
This machine can and will kill us all.
It will survive all of us
It will grind all of us, chew and spit all of us.
And that's capitalism for you.

Ode to sunshine

They will try to break you, to silence you
to invalidate your feelings and gaslight you
They will convince you, that this and that is not
for you, because you are not ready
because you are way over your head
because you are too brown, too soft, too mild,
too shy, too mixed
and your accent is so thick they can barely
understand you
they will try to show you that you don't belong
here
or there or anywhere
They will reserve a place for you out of their
clique, out of their sight
out of their suburbs, out their city, out of their
church,
far from their God.
And yet alone and disenfranchised you'll still be
bright,
you still shine.
Sunshine, don't listen to them.

Light house

I am always navigating through night, dark
water,
violent storms.
Forces of nature,
forces of my nature shake my boat sailing
nowhere,
and despite of your little to no knowledge of
these waters
you keep reminding me of who I am, what I
used to be
with that on my horizon I keep sailing, that
gets me to stop contemplating.
The light that you insist that I have on
and that I no longer see is what keeps me sailing
through darkness.

Behind the scene

I caught a glimpse of you yesterday
while I was driving
I could see your face from far behind the stop
sign
I thought I was dreaming
The sun on the apartments at the end of the road
the leaves of autumn were flying everywhere
so slow and free
the sun was beaming through your head,
crowning you a halo
I thought I was dreaming
If I could cast a spell I would freeze that
moment
to capture all the beauty of that motion picture
It lasted less than a minute.
I would lift the spell to catch a little bit more of
you in motion
behind the stop sign.

True colours

15

On January 6th I understood not without shock,
that hate was normalised,
we all turned into what we fought the most
tyrants, power hungry.
It made me think how naive we all were in the
90's
we did not grasp the depth of the pit
we didn't realise that God was dead
and money took its place.
Disneyworld is the holy land.
No one can save us from greed..
It would have been a Bosch picture, if it wasn't
all over
Fox news.

The past in a cage

When I look back wearing my sincere lenses
nothing was terribly bad, however
I carried that feeling my entire life
A feeling of non belonging
a feeling of not knowing what was for me to do
Some of these children I met in high school have
disappeared ever since
I hope they are still alive.
If they knew the impact of those words, would
they
still repeat them ?
would they still have isolated me ?
It is important to have some strength to navigate
the world
of this cruelty hidden behind the cloak
of an assertive world.

Gutters

You, walking with your signs of
 hate written in your hats,
and pulsing in your heart
angry with the wokeness
and the urge to end injustice.
You are angry for the most part
because your world is slowly ceasing to exist.
You are going out of fashion, obsolete.
The world keeps turning
while you're just sitting, shouting, lurking
spitting out hate on the corners.
I don't hate you, I don't pity you
The world is evolving, but no longer around
you.
You shall pass.

Refugee

Through your eyes I've seen the world you've
left behind
When you move your chin up to align with the
horizon
Full moon behind us
I've heard sounds and words I could not name it
yet
You left behind the fragrance of the (national
flower)
Will that still bloom again?
You left the fragrances of all spices, homemade
meals meant to be cherished
With family, meals that fed your soul
For fast food
You left behind the murmur of the Congo River
and the majesty of the banks it touched
Will the violet turaco bird still there? if so, for
whom to, see?
You left the sacred soil of your homeland,
stepped by generations to land here
Running away from the senseless war,
You left behind the beauty of nature
The force of your traditions
The sound of your languages
The unity of being one with your people

The sacredness of your ancestors
Keep your chin up
We are all a small part of things bigger than life
itself
Homesickness I know that pain
The tears that roll down from the eyes that long
seeing what was once familiar
Longing
Will the violet turaco bird still be there for
whoever is left to see?

Cloud nine

Grey days like this makes me feel like
running away from me to find me
somewhere else,
where cloud days strolling between the wild
flowers
of summer end
the eyes of my mother,
my father laugh
now that they grew older they are child that I
used to be
free and touching the wild flowers,
absorbed with the birds from the native centre
I am happy I lived enough to see them this way.

Sanctuary

It is important to keep a place
inside that you just don't share with anyone.
An intact interior palace
that no one knows, nor need to fix it nor alter
A place inside that you hold your thoughts, your
songs
your favourite Camus passage
where the winds blows
and you can run free
Sitting still and breathing
the warm breath of solitude.

Fear of missing out

I seem to always return to
the palace my recurring dreams
of shadows and clouds
the smell of afternoons warmed by a touch of
sun
It is peaceful here.
However I still think about you.
An entire part of me misses the part of you that
never took that train,
that never waved goodbye.
I miss the part of you, that did not dismiss me,
that had the courage to make a bet.
I was there when I said I would be.
I fancy thinking that we are happy somewhere
where the parts of us that did not failed
were brave enough to live what we thought it
was out there
for us to live.

Long life

We all wanted to live a little longer,
not only survive the mourns of times.
We all wanted the world to still remember us,
to want us.
This world that so much crucifies, vilifies,
indignifies us.
We wanted reassurance, approval ,sense of
belonging
somehow a testimony that we lived right
that we lived all that had to be lived.
Are there amends to be made ? I am pretty there
are many
we need to find meaning, significance of what
we are living
of what life is about, and if it is about anything
anyways.
However we shall live briefly, not to be
completely forgotten
But to carry the future generations
as our ancestors have been carrying us on our
shoulders.

Advice

It is a very competitive world over what ?
Never thought I'd be the one thinking we've
failed to see the bigger picture
Never knew I would be telling how people will
hurt you,
Friends will betray you and the world sometimes
would split us in two.
When that happens, be on the peacemakers side,
no matter how hard it is.
Your kindness will create waves that you may
not see,
Lift up people when they need it just because
you can.

www.ingramcontent.com/pod-product-compliance
Lightning Source LLC
LaVergne TN
LVHW021338200726
843509LV00014B/2575